ALL ABOUT ME!

Who is The Sugar Rose Kitchen?

Well it's basically just me Samantha Monoyou, assisted by my long-suffering husband, and wonderful family and friends who pitch in when needed to help me out with cake engineering, deliveries, topping huge boxes of cupcakes and working on my stall!

I started the business in 2015, making celebration cakes, specialising in children's cakes with novelty/illusion cakes being my favourite challenge. The business has developed organically to the point where our main business is now making indulgent cupcakes and massive brownies to sell at local businesses, events and markets throughout Gloucestershire. More recently I have launched a postal brownie service where I send a variety of brownie options all over the UK.

I have a huge passion for baking, and for helping others. From chats with friends who were struggling with different aspects of baking I realised there was something I could do to help. That's when the Easy Baking recipe book was born. All the recipes contained in this book are very straightforward. A lot of them work as good bases for experimentation once you've perfected them. I hope you enjoy the book, if you'd like to send me feedback or leave reviews for any recipes you try, I'd really appreciate it*.

Happy baking!

Sam x

All photography throughout this book is by Craig Ballinger Photography

*see last page for contact info.

Sugar Rose

contents

victoria sponge

VICTORIA SPONGE

Makes: 8-10 slices   **Total time:** 45 mins (not incl cooling)

The classic Victoria sponge cake, a firm favourite at afternoon tea. Light, fluffy, melt in the mouth, and...
It's the easiest recipe to remember!

INGREDIENTS

4 medium eggs – room temperature, weighed in their shells, take this measurement and weigh the rest of the ingredients to the same amount (will most likely be between 200-240g).

Butter (softened)
Caster sugar
Self-raising flour
1 tbsp milk

METHOD

- Pre-heat oven to 170°C fan/375°F/gas 5.
- Grease and line two 8" (20cm) sandwich cake tins.
- Cream butter and sugar together with a hand or stand mixer for 3-5 minutes.
- Add the eggs one at a time with a spoonful of the measured flour.
- Gently fold in the remaining flour with a spoon.
- Add the milk and combine.
- Split the mixture evenly between the two tins.
- Bake in the pre-heated oven for 20-25 minutes until lightly golden brown and a cake tester or skewer comes out clean.
- Allow to cool in the tins for 5 minutes then turn out onto a cooling rack.
- Fill with just strawberry jam and a dusting of icing sugar for a traditional Victoria sandwich.

VARIATIONS

1. Try using different jams such as blackcurrant or mixed berry.
2. Add fresh fruit and fresh whipped cream to turn this into more of a dessert.

TOP TIP

Turn this into more of a treat (see photo) by filling with a simple buttercream. Mix together 250g softened butter with 500g icing sugar, 2 tbsp milk and 1 tsp vanilla extract beat with a mixer for 5-10 minutes.

CHOCOLATE SPONGE CAKE

Makes: 8-10 slices   **Total time:** 50 mins (not incl cooling)

This is, in my opinion, the perfect chocolate sponge cake. It is sturdy enough to take the weight of buttercream or fondant icing and other decoration, it bakes flat and is really chocolatey without being like a fudge cake.

INGREDIENTS

For the cake:
250g softened butter
250g caster sugar
5 medium eggs
200g self-raising flour
50g cocoa powder
100g melted milk chocolate

For the buttercream:
250g butter (softened)
500g icing sugar
6 tbsp cocoa powder
2 tbsp boiling water (plus more as needed)
125ml melted milk chocolate

METHOD

For the cake:

- Pre-heat oven to 160°C fan/350°F/Gas 4.
- Grease and line two 8" (20cm) cake tins.
- Melt the milk chocolate in the microwave or in a heatproof bowl over a saucepan of boiling water.
- Mix all of the ingredients together (you can also use the creaming method but I find the warm chocolate helps everything combine easily with the all-in-one method).
- Split the mixture between the two lined cake tins, give them a tap on the worktop to release any air bubbles before popping into the oven.
- Bake for 25-30 minutes or until a skewer or cake tester comes out clean.
- Take the cakes out of the oven and leave them to cool in the tins for 5-10 minutes.
- Remove the cakes from their tins and pop them onto a cooling rack to cool completely.

For the buttercream:

- Cream butter and half the icing sugar together until light and fluffy.
- Add the remaining icing sugar, cocoa and melted chocolate. Mix until combined.
- Add the boiling water to loosen the mixture, mix until smooth.
- Sandwich in between the sponges then cover the sides and top.

VARIATIONS

1. Try using different jams such as blackcurrant or mixed berry.
2. Add fresh fruit and fresh whipped cream to turn this into more of a dessert.

TOP TIP

Turn this into more of a treat (see photo) by filling with a simple buttercream. Mix together 250g softened butter with 500g icing sugar, 2 tbsp milk and 1 tsp vanilla extract beat with a mixer for 5-10 minutes.

chocolate sponge

carrot cake

CARROT CAKE

Makes: 8-10 slices   **Total time:** 1.5 hrs (not incl cooling)

A tea time favourite, with a rich, tangy cream cheese frosting.

INGREDIENTS

For the cake:

450ml sunflower oil
400g plain flour
2 tsp bicarbonate of soda
550g caster sugar
5 eggs
Pinch of salt
2½ tsp cinnamon
525g carrots, peeled and grated
Zest of 1 orange (optional)

For the cream cheese frosting:

270g full fat cream cheese
70g butter
290g icing sugar
½ tsp orange extract (optional)

METHOD

For the cake:
- Preheat the oven to 160**°C** fan/350**°F**/Gas 4
- Grease and line (including the sides) an 8" (20cm) deep cake tin.
- Mix all ingredients except the carrots, in a bowl with a wooden spoon.
- Stir in the grated carrots.
- Pour the mixture into the lined cake tin and bake for 1 hour 15 minutes, or until a cake tester or skewer comes out clean.
- Cool in the tin for 10 minutes before taking out of the tin and leaving on a cooling rack until completely cooled.

To decorate:
- To make the frosting, beat the cream cheese, icing sugar and butter together until light and fluffy. Then ice however you wish!
- Use orange and green fondant icing to make carrots. You can do this by hand or use a fondant mould. If using a mould just fill and pop in the freezer for about 15 minutes.

VARIATIONS

1. Add the zest of one orange to the mix and ½ tsp of orange extract to the icing.
2. Add raisins and/or walnuts to the mix to give some extra levels of texture and flavour. About 150g of either will work well.

TOP TIP

Use a food processor to grate the carrots if you have one, it's so much quicker and saves the orange fingers!

COUNTRY FRUIT CAKE

Makes: 8-10 slices   **Total time:** 1.5 hrs (not incl cooling)

A rustic and traditional cake, great for picnics or with a big mug of tea, it is comforting and really easy to make. This is easily the quickest cake to prepare but the longest to bake!

INGREDIENTS

550g dried fruit
170g butter
4 eggs
80ml milk
170g brown sugar
335g self-raising flour
2½ teaspoons mixed spice

METHOD

- Pre-heat oven to 160°C fan/350°F/Gas 4.
- Grease and line an 8" (20cm) deep cake tin.
- Mix all ingredients except the fruit with a hand or stand mixer.
- Add fruit and fold in until evenly distributed.
- Bake for 1 hour 15 minutes.
- Test cake with cake tester or skewer, if it comes out clean the cake is ready

VARIATIONS

1. Decorate the top with a glaze made from 2 tbsp apricot jam gently warmed in a saucepan and add fruit such as glace cherries, nuts such as walnuts or pecans.
2. Add cherries or chopped apricots to the recipe for a little juicy surprise!

TOP TIP

If the cake starts to brown on top before it's ready, turn the oven temperature down slightly and cover the top of the cake with a circle of foil.

country fruit cake

LEMON DRIZZLE MADEIRA LOAF

Makes: 9 slices   **Total time:** 1 hr 10 mins (not incl cooling)

Most lemon drizzle recipes use a traditional sponge like the Victoria but I personally prefer a Madeira style cake. This was one of my dear old Dad's favourite cakes of mine, and he was a chocoholic so that's praise indeed for a lemon cake!

INGREDIENTS

225g butter
225g caster sugar
4 eggs
340g self-raising flour
4 tbsp milk
2 lemons (zested and 1½ juiced
– the juice is for the drizzle)
125g granulated sugar, also for
the drizzle

METHOD

- Preheat the oven to 160°C fan/350°F/Gas 4.
- Grease and line a 900g/2lb loaf tin.
- Cream butter and sugar together with a hand or stand mixer for 3-5 minutes.
- Add the eggs one at a time with a spoonful of the measured flour.
- Gently fold in the remaining flour and the lemon zest with a spoon.
- Add the milk and combine.
- Pour the cake batter into the lined loaf tin.
- Bake in the pre-heated oven for 45-55 minutes until lightly golden brown and a cake tester or skewer comes out clean. Depending on your oven it could take longer.
- Allow to cool in the tin for 10 minutes.
- Meanwhile, stir together the lemon juice and granulated sugar. Poke holes in the cake using a skewer. Pour the icing over the cake whilst still in the tin. Leave to cool.

VARIATIONS

1. Add orange or lime zest and juice to the lemon to mix things up a bit.
2. Swap the lemon for orange and add a few tablespoons of prosecco to the drizzle to turn this into a grown-up boozy bucks fizz cake!

TOP TIP

Be sure to line the tin very well or when you pour the drizzle over it could stick to the tin and make it hard to get the cake out!

lemon drizzle

classic brownie

CLASSIC BROWNIE

Makes: 12 portions . **Total time:** 50 mins (not incl cooling)

Another great base here, master this and they'll be eating out the palm of your hand... or rather straight from the tin, with a big dollop of ice cream!

INGREDIENTS

r250g dark chocolate
250g butter
350g caster sugar
4 large eggs
125g plain flour
45g cocoa powder
175g milk chocolate chunks

METHOD

- Pre-heat oven to 170°C fan/375°F/Gas 5.
- Grease and line a 9 x 12" (20 x 30cm) brownie tin.
- Melt butter and dark chocolate together on a low heat.
- Whisk sugar and eggs together with a hand or stand mixer (if using a stand mixer, use the whisk attachment).
- Add slightly cooled melted chocolate mixture to the egg mixture and stir to combine.
- Add flour and cocoa to the mixture and fold in.
- Stir in chocolate chunks.
- Bake for approximately 35 minutes.
- Test the brownie, when it's ready a cake tester or skewer will come out slightly moist with some crumbs attached. If it's runny the brownie is undercooked, if it comes out clean it's already overbaked.

VARIATIONS

1. Try adding different chocolate chunks, white, dark etc or drizzling with chocolate.
2. Add 1 tsp of flavouring or extract such as orange or mint.

TOP TIP

Brownies are so versatile, here are some ideas of how to serve them:

1. Chop into small chunks and put in a pretty box or bag to give as a gift.
2. Slice into finger portions for an after school or picnic treat.
3. Serve warmed, with cream or ice cream (salted caramel is really good)!

flapjack

FLAPJACK

Makes: 12 portions   **Total time:** 25 mins (not incl cooling)

A lunchbox favourite! Ready within half an hour.

INGREDIENTS

375g oats (I find standard porridge oats work best)
175g butter
175g light brown sugar
125ml golden syrup

METHOD

- Heat oven to 180°C fan/400°F/Gas 6
- Grease and line a 9 x 12" (20 x 30cm) brownie tin or roasting tray (must be deep)
- Melt the butter and both sugars with the golden syrup slowly over a low heat stirring regularly.
- Take off the heat and stir in the oats.
- Pour into the prepared tin, spread out and flatten with the back of the spoon.
- Bake in the oven for 15 minutes, checking halfway through in case your oven heat is uneven (you may need to turn the tray around).
- Take out of the oven and pop the tin on to a cooling rack.
- Take a knife and carefully mark into 12 squares (or however many you would like) then leave to cool in the tin.
- STUFF YOUR FACE WITH GOOEY LOVELINESS!

VARIATIONS

1. Add chocolate chips or dip in chocolate.
2. Swap the golden syrup for honey or maple syrup for a completely different flavour.

TOP TIP

You can choose gluten free oats if you need to, for an easy switch.

ROCKY ROAD

Makes: 12 slices   **Total time:** 20 mins (not incl chilling)

A no-bake wonder that the kids will absolutely love. One of my personal favourites, I'll just chuck anything in!

INGREDIENTS

270g butter
400g 70% dark chocolate
4-6 tbsp golden syrup
300g rich tea or digestive biscuits
200g mini marshmallows plus extra for topping (chopped regular marshmallows work well too)
I also added 50g fudge chunks and 50g raisins

METHOD

- Grease and line a 9 x 12" (20 x 30cm) brownie tin.
- Smash up biscuits into small chunks with a rolling pin and put to one side.
- Melt butter, chocolate and golden syrup on a low heat.
- Leave to cool for five minutes.
- Stir the smashed biscuits and marshmallows (and any other ingredients you might be adding) into the melted chocolate mix.
- Sprinkle some extra marshmallows on top.
- Pop the tray into the fridge and chill for 2-3 hours.

VARIATIONS

1. Try different additions such as cherries, nuts, cranberries, honeycomb.
2. You can also try different chocolate; white chocolate rocky road is delicious!

TOP TIP

I use a cereal bag to put the biscuits in before smashing them, as they're hard wearing and don't tend to rip.

rocky road

blondie

WHITE CHOCOLATE BLONDIE

Makes: 12 slices   **Total time:** 50 mins

I often get asked what a blondie is. Basically, it's a similar bake to a brownie but instead of melting dark chocolate and adding cocoa powder it relies on brown sugar to give it it's richness. Blondies can have white, milk or dark chocolate chips but in this instance, I use white chocolate in the same way I would use dark chocolate in a brownie. This method has created the perfect blondie in my opinion!

INGREDIENTS

240g white chocolate
260g butter
240g brown sugar
80g caster sugar
3 eggs
200g plain flour
2½ teaspoons vanilla extract

METHOD

- Pre-heat oven to 170°C/375°F/gas 5.
- Grease and line a 9 x 12" (20 x 30cm) brownie tin.
- Melt butter and half of the white chocolate together on a low heat.
- Whisk both sugars and the eggs together with a hand or stand mixer.
- Add slightly cooled melted white chocolate mixture to the egg mixture and stir to combine.
- Add flour and vanilla extract to the mixture and fold in.
- Chop the remaining white chocolate into small chunks (or use chocolate chunks or chips). Add to the mixture and stir in.
- Bake for approximately 35 minutes.
- Test the blondie, when it's ready a cake tester or skewer will come out slightly moist with some crumbs attached. If it's runny the blondie is undercooked, if it comes out clean it's already overbaked.

VARIATIONS

1. Swap out the vanilla extract for something different such as coconut or almond flavouring. Add cherries, cranberries, nuts. Whatever takes your fancy!
2. Swap the white chocolate chunks at the end for milk or dark chocolate or a combination of two or even all three!

TOP TIP

A blondie should be a little fudgy, like a brownie. Though it does still taste delicious if it comes out cakey too!

VANILLA SPRINKLE TRAYBAKE

Makes: 12 slices   **Total time:** 45 mins (not incl cooling)

Here's a retro classic for you!
Perfect for parties, this is an easy birthday traybake for a big crowd or just a teatime treat. It's so easy to make and decorate, and completely delicious.

INGREDIENTS

For the traybake:
240g butter (softened)
240g caster sugar
5 eggs
300g self-raising flour
5 tbsp milk
1 tsp vanilla extract

For the icing:
400g icing sugar
8 tbsp milk
50g sprinkles

METHOD

- Pre-heat oven to 140°C fan/275°F/Gas 1.
- Grease and line a 9 x 12" (20 x 30cm) brownie tin.
- Cream butter and sugar together with a hand mixer or stand mixer.
- Add eggs one by one with a tbsp of flour each time.
- Fold in the rest of the flour.
- Add the milk and vanilla.
- Pour into the lined tray and bake for 25-30 minutes, until a cake tester or skewer comes out clean.
- Leave to cool completely then carefully turn out of the tin.
- Mix the icing sugar and milk together. Pour it onto the cake and spread carefully with a spatula. Then it's time to completely cover the cake in sprinkles!

VARIATIONS

You could adapt this cake by adding lemon or orange zest (or both!) and flavouring the icing with extract or mixing lemon juice with the icing instead of milk.

TOP TIP

Try and avoid the temptation to lift the cake out before it's completely cool or it might break.

vanilla sprinkle

cupcakes

CLASSIC VANILLA CUPCAKE

Makes: 12 cupcakes   **Total time:** 40 mins (not incl cooling)

My basic cupcake, one of my best sellers to grown-ups and kids alike! No filling, no fuss, just a great tasting light sponge with a generous portion of yummy buttercream!

INGREDIENTS

For the cupcake:
150g butter (softened)
150g caster sugar
3 eggs
150g self-raising flour
1/4 tsp baking powder
3/4 teaspoon vanilla

For the buttercream:
250g butter (softened)
500g icing sugar
2 tbsp milk
1 tsp vanilla extract

METHOD

For the cupcakes:
- Prepare a 12-hole cupcake tray with baking cases (paper or silicone).
- Pre-heat oven to 160**°C** fan/350**°F**/gas 4.
- Cream butter and sugar together using a hand mixer or stand mixer.
- Sieve flour and baking powder together into a bowl.
- Add each egg individually with a spoonful of flour per egg and mix until combined.
- Stir with a spoon to fold in the rest of the flour and the vanilla extract.
- Using an ice cream scoop divide the mixture between the cupcake cases.
- Bake for 15 minutes or until a cake tester or skewer comes out clean.
- Leave to cool in the tin for 5 minutes then lift out onto a cooling rack.
- Once completely cooled ice with buttercream and add some sprinkles.

For the buttercream:
- Mix together the softened butter, icing sugar, milk and vanilla extract, beat with a mixer for 5-10 minutes.
- Fill a piping bag (fitted with a nozzle) with the buttercream and make sure there are no air bubbles.
- Pipe the buttercream on top of the cakes (see TOP TIP below)

VARIATIONS

1. Add a teaspoon of jam to the inside of the cupcakes. Any flavour you fancy.
2. Experiment with different buttercream flavours and sprinkles.

TOP TIP

When piping the buttercream, fill the icing bag well and squeeze out any air bubbles. Then pipe your swirl holding the icing bag completely straight down, work from the inside out (stop here if you want a rose effect) then back round again to get back to the middle (for a large swirl).

CHOCOLATE CUPCAKE

Makes: 12 cupcakes   **Total time:** 45 mins (not incl cooling)

This is one of my favourite recipes, these cakes are light and melt in the mouth, but also super chocolatey and rich! Lovely served with a drizzle of cream!

INGREDIENTS

For the cupcakes:
150g self-raising flour
233g caster sugar
2 tbsp cocoa powder
130ml buttermilk
90ml water
50ml vegetable oil
1 egg

For the buttercream:
250g butter (softened)
500g icing sugar
5 tbsp cocoa powder
2 tbsp boiling water

METHOD

For the cakes:
- Prepare a 12-hole cupcake tray with baking cases (paper or silicone).
- Pre-heat oven to 160C fan/350°F/Gas 4.
- Whisk flour, sugar, baking powder, bicarbonate of soda and salt together into a large bowl.
- Add eggs, water, coffee extract and buttermilk to the dry ingredients and stir.
- Portion out into the cupcake cases using an ice cream scoop for an even portion.
- Bake for 20 minutes or until a cake tester or skewer comes out clean.
- Leave to cool in the tray for five minutes.
- Pop on a cooling rack to cool completely whilst you make the buttercream.

For the buttercream:
- Cream butter and half the icing sugar together until light and fluffy.
- Add the remaining icing sugar and cocoa and continue to mix until fully combined.
- Add boiling water to loosen the mixture, mix until smooth.
- Fill a piping bag (fitted with a nozzle) with the buttercream and make sure there are no air bubbles.
- Pipe the buttercream on top of the cakes (see TOP TIP in vanilla cupcake recipe).

VARIATIONS

1. Try some chocolate and hazelnut spread as a filling for the cupcakes, then replace 50g of the butter with the spread in the buttercream for a delicious chocolate and hazelnut cupcake.
2. Add some orange zest and orange juice in the buttercream instead of water.

TOP TIP

If you can't get hold of buttermilk you can simply make your own by adding half a tablespoon of lemon juice to the 130ml milk. Leave for a few minutes to rest and curdle before adding to the cake mix.

chocolate

vanilla and blackcurrant

VANILLA and BLACKCURRANT

Makes: 12 cupcakes   **Total time:** 40 mins (not incl cooling)

A slight adjustment to the classic vanilla cake can make something really special! Vanilla and blackcurrant are a delicious combination.

INGREDIENTS

For the cupcake:
150g butter (softened)
150g caster sugar
3 eggs
150g self-raising flour
1/4 tsp baking powder
3/4 tsp vanilla

For the buttercream:
250g butter (softened)
500g icing sugar
3 tbsp blackcurrant jam (plus 12 tsp for the filling)
1 tsp vanilla extract

METHOD

For the cupcakes:
- Prepare a 12-hole cupcake tray with baking cases (paper or silicone).
- Pre-heat oven to 160C fan/350°F/gas 4.
- Cream butter and caster sugar together using a hand or stand mixer.
- Add each egg individually with a spoonful of flour per egg and stir to combine.
- Stir with a spoon to fold in the rest of the flour.
- Using an ice cream scoop divide the mixture between the cupcake cases.
- Bake for 15 minutes or until a cake tester or skewer comes out clean.
- Leave to cool in the tin for five minutes then lift out onto a cooling rack.
- Once cooled fill with blackcurrant jam. Use a cupcake corer to make a hole in the middle of the cake and fill with a teaspoon of jam. Replace the cake core.

For the buttercream:
- Mix together the softened butter and icing sugar.
- Add the milk and vanilla and beat with a mixer for 5 minutes until smooth.
- Add the blackcurrant jam and gently stir into the buttercream.
- Fill a piping bag (fitted with a nozzle) with the buttercream and make sure there are no air bubbles.
- Pipe the buttercream on top of the cakes (see TOP TIP below).

VARIATIONS

1. Add some fresh blackcurrants to the cake mix and top the cupcake with them too.
2. Turn it into a blackcurrant cheesecake cupcake by making a biscuit base using melted butter and digestive biscuits before adding the cake mix on top then add some cream cheese to the buttercream.

TOP TIP

Use a wide or round nozzle for the buttercream or small bits of blackberry might get caught in the nozzle and cause the buttercream to back up and not pipe properly.

STICKY TOFFEE CUPCAKE

Makes: 12 cupcakes

Total time: 35 mins (not incl cooling)
Plus 30 mins soaking time.

This cupcake uses dates and brown sugar to create the flavour. Topped with a toffee flavoured buttercream it's the ideal pudding themed cake!

INGREDIENTS

For the cake:
180g chopped dates
80g butter (softened)
150g light brown sugar
2 eggs
180g plain white flour
1 tsp bicarbonate of soda
1/2 tsp salt

For the buttercream:
250g butter (softened)
500g icing sugar
2 tbsp toffee sauce

To decorate:
toffee sauce
fudge chunks to decorate

METHOD

For the cupcakes:
- Place the dates in a heatproof bowl and cover with 150ml boiling water. Leave for 30 minutes to soften.
- Prepare a 12-hole cupcake tray with baking cases (paper or silicone).
- Pre-heat oven to 160C fan/350°F/gas 4.
- Cream butter and light brown sugar together using a hand mixer or stand mixer.
- Sieve flour, bicarbonate of soda and salt together into a bowl.
- Add each egg individually with a spoonful of flour per egg and stir to combine.
- Fold in the rest of the flour with a spoon.
- Add the date and water mixture and fold in until combined.
- Using an ice cream scoop divide the mixture between the cupcake cases.
- Bake for 20 minutes or until a cake tester or skewer comes out clean.
- Leave to cool in the tin for 5 minutes then lift out onto a cooling rack.
- Once completely cooled ice with buttercream and top with toffee sauce and fudge.

For the buttercream:
- Mix together the softened butter and icing sugar, beat for 5 minutes until smooth.
- Add the toffee and swirl through the buttercream.
- Fill a piping bag (with a nozzle) with the buttercream and squeeze out any air bubbles.
- Pipe the buttercream on top of the cakes (see TOP TIP in vanilla cupcake recipe).
- Finish off with a sprinkling of fudge pieces and another drizzle of toffee sauce.

VARIATIONS

1. Core and fill the cupcakes with toffee sauce too for a luxurious surprise inside!
2. Reduce the amount of butter and some custard to the buttercream.

TOP TIP

The brown sugar in this recipe makes this a very dark sponge, it can look cooked before it's actually ready.

sticky toffee

caramel biscuit

CARAMEL BISCUIT CUPCAKE

Makes: 12 cupcakes   **Total time:** 35 mins (not incl cooling)

If you haven't discovered caramelised biscuit spread yet you're in for a treat! It is incredible in this cupcake. Swapping caster sugar for brown instantly turns the cupcake into a rich caramel flavour to complement the filling and buttercream.

INGREDIENTS

For the cupcakes:
150g butter
150g light brown sugar
3 eggs
150g self-raising flour (sieved)
1/2 tsp baking powder

For the buttercream:
150g butter (softened)
300g icing sugar
200g caramel biscuit spread (plus an extra 12 tsp for the filling)
1-2 tbsp water

METHOD

For the cupcakes:
- Prepare a 12-hole cupcake tray with baking cases (paper or silicone).
- Pre-heat oven to 160C fan/350°F/gas 4.
- Cream butter and brown sugar together using a hand mixer or stand mixer.
- Add each egg individually with a spoonful of flour per egg and mix until combined.
- Stir with a spoon to fold in the rest of the flour.
- Using an ice cream scoop divide the mixture between the cupcake cases.
- Bake for 15 minutes or until a cake tester or skewer comes out clean.
- Leave to cool in the tin for 5 minutes then lift out onto a cooling rack.
- Once completely cooled fill with caramel biscuit spread. Use a cupcake corer to make a hole in the middle of the cake and fill with a teaspoon of spread. Replace the cake core.
- Ice with buttercream and top with a caramel biscuit for the full effect.

For the buttercream:
- Mix together the softened butter, icing sugar and caramelised biscuit spread.
- Add the water and beat with a mixer for 5 minutes until smooth.
- Fill a piping bag (with a nozzle) with buttercream and squeeze out any air bubbles.
- Pipe the buttercream on top of the cakes (see TOP TIP in vanilla cupcake recipe).

VARIATIONS

1. Add some toffee sauce and biscuit crumbs as a drizzle on top.
2. Make a base for the cupcakes by mixing biscuit crumbs and butter and lining the bottom of the cupcake cases before adding the cake mix.

TOP TIP

Always leave the baked cupcakes in the tin for 5 minutes before removing and popping on a cooling rack. If you try and remove too early, they'll crumble, too long and they may sink, or the cases may peel off.

CHOCOLATE CHIP COOKIES

Makes: 12-15 cookies   **Total time:** 20 mins (not incl cooling)

These always disappear so quickly in my house! It's taken a bit of trial and error to get the perfect chocolate chip cookie. You can roll up this dough and chop circles off to bake or use an ice cream scoop (if you've made any recipes from the cupcake section, you'll know how fond of this tool I am!).

INGREDIENTS

150g butter
80g brown sugar
80g granulated sugar
2 tsp vanilla extract
1 large egg yolk
225g plain flour
1/2 tsp bicarbonate of soda
1/4 tsp salt
100g chocolate chunks

METHOD

- Line two cookie sheets or baking trays with baking paper or silicone tray liners.
- Heat the oven to 170°C fan/375°F/gas 5.
- Beat butter and both sugars together with a hand mixer until light and fluffy.
- Beat in vanilla extract and egg.
- Add plain flour, bicarbonate of soda and salt to the bowl
- Mix well with a wooden spoon.
- Add chocolate chips or chunks and stir well.
- Use an ice cream scoop to make rounds of the mixture, spacing them well apart on the baking trays. This mixture should make about 12-15 cookies.
- Bake for 8–10 mins until they are light brown on the edges and still slightly soft in the centre if you press them.
- Leave on the tray for a couple of mins to set and then lift onto a cooling rack.

VARIATIONS

1. Of course different chocolate chips, nuts and fudge chunks can all be added, maybe experiment with one at a time.
2. Try some flavourings, just 1/2 tsp per mixture. Chocolate orange is a particular favourite.

TOP TIP

This mixture freezes really well, it's great recipe to prep before Christmas, make dough well ahead of time. Freeze and pull out portions of dough as and when you would like to bake them.

SHORTBREAD

Makes: 12-15 biscuits   **Total time:** 20 mins (not incl cooling)

A yummy buttery shortbread recipe which once perfected, can be used as a great base for lots of different flavour combinations.

INGREDIENTS

125g butter
55g caster sugar
180g plain flour

METHOD

- Line a cookie sheet with baking paper (or a silicone baking liner).
- Cream butter and sugar together until light and fluffy.
- Add flour and mix until a smooth dough forms.
- Roll out dough to 1cm thick and cut into whatever shape you like.
- Lay the dough shapes onto your tray.
- Chill for 20 minutes.
- Pre-heat oven to 170°C fan/375°F/gas 5.
- Bake for 15-20 minutes.
- Cool on the tray for five minutes then carefully transfer to a cooling rack.

VARIATIONS

1. Add chocolate chips and fruit to the mix. White chocolate and cranberry are a favourite combination of mine.
2. Try some unusual flavour combinations such as lemon and rosemary, delish!

TOP TIP

Try not to knead the dough too much, the more it's worked the less 'short' the pastry will be and you'll lose the crumbly texture that shortbread is well known for.

shortbread

OAT AND RAISIN COOKIES

Makes: 12-15 cookies   **Total time:** 20 mins (not incl cooling)
Plus 15 mins soaking time

A great everyday cookie; thick, chewy and delicious!

INGREDIENTS

100g raisins
50ml boiling water
200g golden caster sugar
150ml sunflower oil
1 large egg (beaten)
1tsp cinnamon or ginger
140g plain flour
1/4 tsp bicarbonate of soda
pinch salt
300g oats

METHOD

- Pre-heat oven to 160°C fan/350°F/Gas 4.
- Line a cookie sheet or baking tray with baking paper.
- Cover raisins with boiling water and leave for 15 minutes.
- In the meantime, using a hand mixer combine the sugar and oil in a large bowl.
- Add the egg and mix.
- Add the flour, spices, bicarbonate of soda and salt and mix with a spoon.
- Add the raisins and water, mix and then add the oats.
- Combine all of the ingredients together.
- Portion out cookies onto the cookie sheet or tray leaving a 2" space between them.
- Bake in the oven for 12-15 minutes. The larger the cookie the more time you'll need.
- Leave to cool on the tray for five minutes, then carefully transfer to a cooling rack.

VARIATIONS

This recipe is dairy free. In addition it can be easily adapted to gluten free with gluten free flour and oats. It can also be made vegan by replacing the egg with a flax egg.

TOP TIP

When portioning out the dough, use a tablespoon for 24 standard sized cookies, or an ice cream scoop for 12 perfectly portioned large, soft cookies.

oat and raisin cookies

SUGAR COOKIES

Makes: 15-20 depending on size of cutter   **Total time:** 20 mins
(not incl. cooling) Plus 40-50 mins chilling time

A super versatile recipe which can be cut into any shape and decorated in many different ways. Everyday treats for the biscuit barrel or something really special as a gift. Be prepared for some waiting around with this one, the dough needs chilling in the fridge twice.

INGREDIENTS

225g butter
200g caster sugar
1 tsp vanilla extract
1 egg, beaten
250g plain flour
1/4 tsp baking powder
1/4 tsp salt

METHOD

- Line a cookie sheet with baking paper (or a silicone baking liner).
- Whisk flour and baking powder together
- Cream butter and sugar with a hand mixer or stand mixer until light and fluffy
- (about three minutes).
- Add the egg, mixing on a low speed.
- Add the flour and fold in with a spoon until the mix turns into dough. It will be quite sticky.
- Wrap the dough in cling film and chill in the fridge for 20 minutes.
- Roll out the dough to 1/4" thick, cut shapes and place on prepared cookie tray.
- Chill again for another 20-30 minutes.
- Pre-heat oven to 170°C fan/375°F/gas 5.
- Bake for 10-12 minutes or until turning golden brown.

VARIATIONS

V1. You can keep these cookies plain or decorate with icing, and lots of sprinkles.
2. Dip into melted chocolate.

TOP TIP

Flour your work surface really well when rolling out the dough as it will easily stick.

sugar cookies

gingerbread

GINGERBREAD

Makes: 10-12 cookies   **Total time:** 30 mins (not incl cooling)

Oh gingerbread!
Spicy, sturdy, crunchy, so deliciously moreish. Get ready for some serious Christmas vibes with this little beauty!

INGREDIENTS

For the gingerbread:
350g plain flour
1 tsp bicarbonate of soda
2 tsp ground ginger
1 tsp cinnamon
125g butter
175g light brown sugar
1 egg
4 tbsp golden syrup

For the icing:
250g icing sugar
1 tbsp water

METHOD

- Line a cookie sheet with baking paper (or a silicone baking liner).
- Place flour, bicarb, ginger and cinnamon into a food processor and whizz up quickly.
- Add butter to processor and mix until it looks like breadcrumbs.
- Add sugar and mix to combine.
- Beat egg and syrup together with a hand whisk and add to the processor. Mix until it turns into dough.
- Wrap in clingfilm or a beeswax wrap and chill for 15 minutes in the fridge.
- Pre-heat oven to 170**°C**/375**°F**/gas 5.
- Roll out to ¼ thickness and cut whichever shapes you like.
- Bake for 12-15 minutes.
- Allow to cool for 5 minutes on the tray, then transfer to a cooling rack.
- Wait until completely cooled before icing.
- To ice, mix together the icing sugar and water and fill a piping bag (with a small hole piping tip inserted) with the icing.
- The next bit takes practice but if you have a steady hand you're halfway there.
- Pop them on a plate and watch them disappear!

VARIATIONS

1. Once you've perfected the recipe you can try and use a template or cutters for making a gingerbread house!
2. Add a bit of lemon extract to the icing for a tasty tang.

TOP TIP

Practice a bit with the icing to make sure you have the right consistency to pipe with.

CAKE POPS

Makes: 12 cake pops   **Total time:** Over 1hr (including making the cake! Not incl chill time

What to do with leftover cake, cake that's a bit stale, shop-bought cake that's past it's best... make CAKE POPS. My daughter absolutely adores these balls of sweetness, but only if the icing is pink!

INGREDIENTS

For the cake:
120g butter
120g caster sugar
120g self-raising flour
2 medium eggs

For the buttercream:
75g butter
150g icing sugar
1/2 tsp vanilla extract
1/2 tbsp milk

To decorate:
200g chocolate or candy melts
50g sprinkles

METHOD

- Make the cake and the buttercream (see Victoria Sponge recipe for instructions). Or use leftover cake.
- Once the cake is cooled, crumble it up and mix with the buttercream.
- Take tablespoons of the cake mixture and roll into balls, transferring each ball to a lined tray or plate then chill for 15 minutes in the fridge.
- In the meantime, melt a small amount of the chocolate or candy melts in the microwave for 1 minute, then in 10second increments until fully melted (or in a heatproof bowl over a saucepan of boiling water, just make sure the bowl doesn't touch the water).
- Take the chilled balls out of the fridge, take the cake pop sticks and dip the ends into the melted chocolate/candy melts individually then insert them into each ball of cake.
- Put the cake pops back in the fridge with the sticks facing upwards.
- Chill for another 30 minutes until the sticks have set hard into the cake balls.
- Melt the rest of the chocolate/candy melts.
- Take the cake pops out of the fridge, dip each one into the chocolate/candy melts, giving them a little turn to coat completely. Allow them to drip a little over the bowl.
- Add some sprinkles, then stand upright either in a cake pop stand or in a mug or glass. Make sure they're not touching and leave them to set for an hour.

VARIATIONS

Use literally any cake flavour combined with any buttercream. Whatever you fancy!
2. Use a popsicle mould and decorate with edible jewels and chocolate drizzle for a really stylish treat.

TOP TIP

Make sure your melted chocolate or candy melts aren't too thick, you can always add a second coat if necessary but if it goes on too thick to start with it will be difficult to work with.

COCONUT ICE

Makes: 20-30 pieces   **Total time:** 10 mins (not incl chill time)

The 1980's called; they want their candy back! I love this stuff and it's insanely quick and easy to make. It's the perfect gift for a coconut lover, in a bag, box or pretty glass jar.

INGREDIENTS

500g condensed milk
500g icing sugar
400g desiccated coconut
A few drops pink edible food colouring or gel colour (or any other colour you fancy!)

METHOD

- Grease and line an 8" (20cm) square baking tin or dish.
- Mix condensed milk and icing sugar together until combined.
- Add the coconut and mix well.
- Split the mixture into two.
- Add the food colouring to one half and mix well (the mixture will be quite stiff at this point so you may have to knead with your hands to distribute the food colouring).
- Layer the white mixture then the pink mixture into the dish and chill for at least 3 hours, preferably overnight.
- Turn out of the dish, cut into squares and dust with icing sugar.

VARIATIONS

1. Try using different food colouring for different batches, multi-coloured pastel coconut ice would make a lovely sweet nibble for a party.
2. Dip the coconut ice chunks in chocolate for an extra treat!

TOP TIP

Clean the knife between cuts to stop the white and pink icing merging together.

coconut ice

chocolate truffles

CHOCOLATE TRUFFLES

Makes: 15-20 truffles   **Total time:** 15 mins (not incl chill time)

Delicious and indulgent chocolate truffles are easier to make than you think, this quick recipe is a basic ganache. The same mix can also be used to fill and cover a chocolate cake just like the one in this book.

INGREDIENTS

300ml double cream
300g 70% dark chocolate
100g chocolate vermicelli (sprinkles)

METHOD

- Break up the chocolate and put into a heatproof bowl.
- Heat the cream on the hob until simmering.
- Add the hot cream to the chocolate and stir until completely melted.
- Chill the mixture until you can mould it with your fingers, about an hour.
- Take tablespoons of the ganache and roll into balls, then coat with sprinkles.
- Pop into a pretty box and give as a fab gift, or scoff them all yourself!

VARIATIONS

1. Experiment by adding some flavourings (orange, mint, rum!).
2. Try different coatings such as cocoa powder, nuts or melted chocolate.

TOP TIP

Use chocolate chips or break the chocolate into really small pieces so it melts more easily when the hot cream is poured on.

CHOCOLATE FUDGE

Makes: 20-25 pieces   **Total time:** 10 mins (not incl chill time)

Rich, luxurious and delicious. This recipe uses ingredients you may already have in the cupboard. There are two very easy methods you can use to make it, microwave or hob.

INGREDIENTS

340g dark chocolate
1 ½ tins condensed milk
1 ½ tsp vanilla flavouring

MICROWAVE METHOD

- Grease and line an 8" (20cm) square baking tin or dish.
- Add chocolate and condensed milk to microwaveable bowl.
- Heat for 1 minute and stir.
- Put back in the microwave for 10 second increments until the chocolate is all melted and the mix is smooth and glossy.
- Add vanilla extract and mix.
- Pour into prepared dish.
- Chill for at least 4 hours but preferably overnight.

HOB METHOD

- Grease and line an 8" (20cm) square baking tin or dish.
- Break up the chocolate and pop into a heatproof bowl.
- Heat the condensed milk until simmering.
- Add the hot milk to the chocolate and stir until all the chocolate has melted.
- Add vanilla extract and mix.
- Pour into prepared dish.
- Chill for at least 4 hours but preferably overnight.

VARIATIONS

1. Add different flavoured extracts such as orange or mint.
2. Add 1 tsp cayenne pepper to the mix to make a warm chilli fudge! (experiment with how much pepper suits your taste).

TOP TIP

Using the hob method, if the chocolate doesn't melt completely when mixing in the cream, pop the heatproof bowl over a saucepan with a couple of inches of boiling water and reheat until it's all melted. Just make sure the water isn't touching the bottom of the bowl or the mix may burn.

chocolate fudge

marshmallow crispy treats

MARSHMALLOW CRISPY TREATS

Makes: 20-30 pieces   **Total time:** 10 - 15 mins
                                           (not incl chill time)

Easy peasy sweet treat for the kids or to give as a gift. So quick to make and super tasty.
I use this mix a lot in celebration cake making too, it's great for sculpting unusual
shapes that set firm but are still really lightweight.

INGREDIENTS

For the treats:
3 tbsp butter
4 cups/200g marshmallows
6 cups/150g rice cereal
1/2 tsp vanilla
Pinch salt

For the topping:
100g chocolate (melted) or candy melts
50g sprinkles

METHOD

- Grease and line a 9 x 12" (20 x 30cm) tin.
- Melt butter and marshmallows in a large saucepan over a low heat or for 2-3
  minutes in the microwave. Stir until all the marshmallows have melted.
- Take off the heat and add the rice cereal. Stir until the cereal is completely coated in
  the marshmallow mixture.
- Coat your hands with oil (coconut is the nicest!) and press mixture into the prepared
  tin.
- Leave to cool.
- Melt chocolate or candy melts and spread across the top of the cereal treats, add
  sprinkles.
- Leave to cool again for the chocolate to set and cut into small squares.

VARIATIONS

1. Of course you can use milk or dark chocolate for the topping, maybe some fudge
chunks instead of sprinkles!
2. Add 1/2 cup of smooth peanut butter towards the end of the melting time and top with
dark chocolate.

TOP TIP

Keep stirring the marshmallows if melting on the hob and keep the heat really low,
they can burn very easily.

equipment

Here is a list of some essential baking equipment you may need:

8" sandwich tins
Hand mixer
Stand mixer
Cake tester
Silicone tin liners
Chocolate melting pot
8" deep tin
Food processor
2lb loaf tin
9 x 12" brownie pan
Three tier cooling rack
Cupcake tin
Cupcake cases
Silicone icing bags
Icing nozzle set for cupcakes
Writing icing nozzle set
Cupcake corer
Cookie sheet
Flour shaker
8" dish
Basic cake decorating kit

Printed in Great Britain
by Amazon

40408910R10034